mameshiba

MEET
MAMESHIBA!

Meet Mameshiba!

Words by **Carrie Shepherd**
Comics by **Gemma Correll**
Design by **Fawn Lau**

Special thanks to
Oscar Charla and **Nami Sato**

Printed in China

Published by VIZ Media, LLC
P.O. Box 77010
San Francisco, CA 94107

10 9 8 7 6 5 4 3 2 1
First printing, July 2011

www.vizkids.com

www.viz.com

What's Mameshiba?

Welcome to the world of **Mameshiba**! These critters look kind of like beans with ears, don't they? In Japanese, **mame** means "bean" and **shiba** is a kind of dog.

Each Mameshiba has its own quirks and personality, and this book lets you know what makes each bean unique! They love sharing random facts with humans, and pop up when you least expect them, so keep your eyes peeled!

Ready?
Without further ado, get ready to meet…

EDAMAME

Bursting with curiosity,
EDAMAME travels around the
world, seeking adventure!

There's no telling where
Edamame will show up next.

Draw Edamame

Follow these steps to draw a PERFECT Edamame!

1. Start with the body!

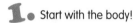

2. Add those eyes that stare into your soul...

3. ...and the signature dog-like mouth!

4. Now ears that hold things as if they were hands...

5. Finally, color Edamame two shades of yummy green!

Try drawing my pod, too!

BLACK BEAN

BLACK BEAN's not much of a conversationalist. This shy bean tends to stare and stare and **STARE**.

And if you look away and Black Bean has disappeared, don't be alarmed— Black Bean also likes to hide.

It's okay to STARE when...

You're in class when you need to look attentive

In a staring contest

Wearing dark glasses (No one can tell!)

Contemplating the freak show at the circus

You're thinking really hard

NATTO

NATTO's a sweaty little bean—and sticky in more ways than one.

Once Natto makes up its mind about something, it sticks to that opinion.

Did you know? Natto is a traditional Japanese food made from fermented soybeans. Try it over rice for a nutritious breakfast–but beware that it has a strong smell!

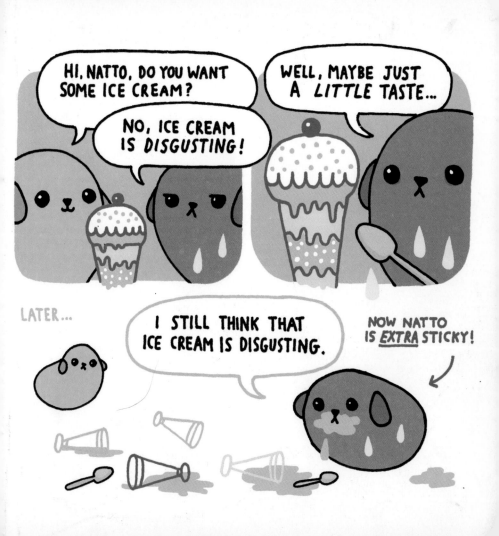

GREEN PEAS

You know that saying "like peas in a pod"? That definitely applies to the GREEN PEAS. They love being together so much, they get nervous if they're ever apart.

Help Green Pea find its friends

Answer:

CHICK-PEA

CHICKPEA is a bit naughty and a bit selfish but, like the Green Peas, hates to be alone.

The many
moods of
Chickpea

PEANUT

FAVA BEAN never flips out. Fava's unflippable— er...*unflappable!*

Ice Cream

Fava Bean loves:

Trivia

Swimming

Lucky clovers

If your love life is bland, CHILI BEAN can help spice things up!

Flowers! Poetry! Soft music! Nothing's too cheesy for this bean in the quest for l'amour!

Did you know?

Your lips are
100 times more sensitive
than your fingertips.

Chili Bean-approved pickup lines

Do you have a GPS? I keep getting lost in your eyes.

Is it Christmas? Looks like Santa left my present right here!

Excuse me, do you have a plum? How about a date?

Do you have a bandage? I got hurt falling for you!

Am I dead? 'Cause it looks like I'm in Heaven right now!

Brr! Let's snuggle up to keep warm!

LENTIL

Need some numbers crunched? LENTIL is a whiz at math and computers.

Just don't hide Lentil's glasses—this bean likes to keep a close eye on things.

Lentil's brain teasers

1. A man needs to get across a river with his **goat**, a **cabbage**, and a **wolf**. His boat will hold him and one other thing. He can't leave the **goat** with the **cabbage** because the goat will eat it. He also can't leave the **wolf** with the **goat**. How does he get all of them across the river?

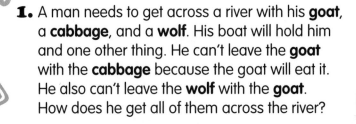

2. A man goes into town on **Friday**. He stays for **three days** and leaves on **Friday**. How?

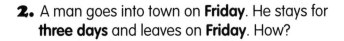

3. What do these four words have in common?
orange   purple   silver   month

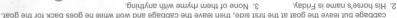

Answers:
1. He should go across once with the goat, go back and get the wolf, take the goat back with him and get the cabbage but leave the goat at the first side, then leave the cabbage and wolf while he goes back for the goat. 2. His horse's name is Friday. 3. None of them rhyme with anything.

TIGER
BEAN

Who comes first with Tiger Bean? TIGER BEAN!

You might want to think twice about lending this rambunctious bean your stuff, because Tiger Bean forgets to return things.

Did you know?

"Tigons" have a tiger father and lioness mother, while "ligers" have a tiger mother and lion father.

RED
BEAN

Smart as a whip and speedy too, RED BEAN is also known for being polite. It's no surprise that this bean is quite popular.

Did you know?

On the island of Java, leaders honor less-powerful people by offering them a half-chewed betel nut.

Politeness around the world

JAPAN 🇯🇵: Never leave your chopsticks sticking upright in your food.

INDIA 🇮🇳: Never reach for food with your left hand. The left hand is used for other tasks, such as cleaning yourself after using the toilet, so it's considered unclean.

AUSTRALIA 🇦🇺: When taking a taxi, sit up front with the driver.

FRANCE 🇫🇷: Always greet the store employees by saying "bonjour."

JAPAN 🇯🇵: It's okay to slurp your noodles.

CHINA 🇨🇳: Always offer your gift with both hands. And if you're receiving a gift, use two hands to accept it as well.

MOROCCO 🇲🇦: Always bargain with merchants.

KENYA 🇰🇪: It's okay to spit when you meet a Masai tribesman. You can do it again when you're leaving.

ARGENTINA 🇦🇷: Cross your knife and fork to show that you're done eating.

CASHEW NUT

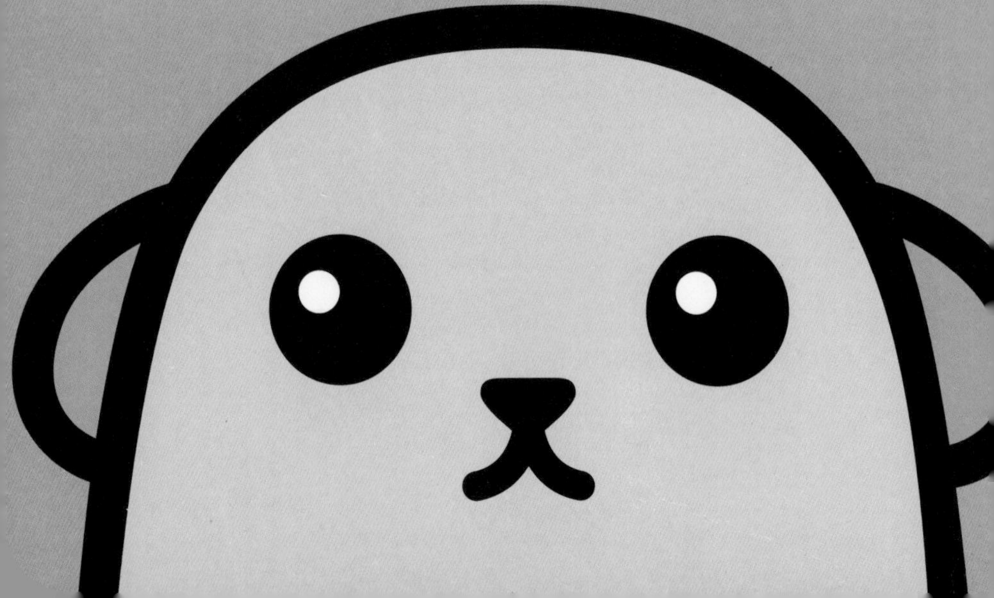

CASHEW NUT is a bit of a rebel who sometimes says things that rub others the wrong way.

Did you know?

Instead of toilets, medieval castles had wooden seats built over a long chute that fed into a moat.

How to make others uncomfortable

Whine loudly when things don't go exactly your way.

Tell someone they look tired. Or sick.

Talk about your digestive troubles in graphic detail.

Borrow money repeatedly and never offer to pay it back.

Wear crazily inappropriate clothing, such as a bikini when it's freezing out, or ripped jeans and a stained T-shirt to a wedding.

Whenever someone talks about an experience or accomplishment, outdo them by telling about your more fabulous experience or accomplishment.

COCOA BEAN

If you want to pull one over on **COCOA BEAN**, you'll probably succeed. Cocoa will believe just about anything!

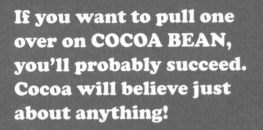

You'll often see Cocoa Bean with Almond— they're best friends.

Did you know? Cocoa beans are also called cacao [ke-kow] beans and are used for making chocolate.

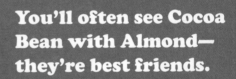

True or false?

1. Chocolate contains a substance that can make people feel like they're falling in love. ■ True ■ False

2. Chocolate causes zits. ■ True ■ False

3. Chocolate is poisonous to dogs. ■ True ■ False

4. White chocolate isn't really chocolate. ■ True ■ False

5. The scientific name for a cacao tree, the obroma, means "food of the gods." ■ True ■ False

LOVE

How many did you get correct?
Turn this around for the answers below!

It's hard to get this Mameshiba
to relax—ALMOND is really uptight!

Good thing this Mameshiba
is friends with Cocoa—
chocolate reduces stress!

Things that irritate Almond

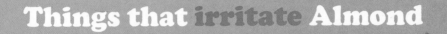

Pointing out that Almond is uptight

Lists

Character guides

Bad jokes

Buzzing mosquitoes

Silly books

Summarizing someone's characteristics
in a couple sentences

Comics

Bad cooking

BLACK-
EYED PEA

BLACK-EYED PEA is one of the newest members of the Mameshiba family. With this bean, there's no in-between—only extremes.

Did you know?

Astronauts are not allowed to eat beans in space because beans cause farting, which damages the space suits.

SOYBEAN

SOYBEAN is a health nut who worries about everyone and everything.

Just like most of our moms, this bean likes to give unsolicited advice.

WHITE SOYBEAN

Pure of heart and a true poet, WHITE SOYBEAN has complete faith in everyone.

*Through good and bad times
Doubt not Mameshiba friends
A pure soul trusts all*

BLACK SOYBEAN

**Baseball? Check.
Swimming? Check.
Curling? Check.**

**You probably can't
come up with a
sport that BLACK
SOYBEAN doesn't
like. This athletic
bean is likely to stay
healthy forever—its
willpower is as
strong as its abs.**

BOILED
BEAN

CRANBERRY BEAN

BOILED BEAN always looks fresh from the boil! A compassionate sort, Boiled Bean is very helpful.

If you like stiff competition, you might want to challenge CRANBERRY BEAN to a game or athletic event.

But beware: Cranberry Bean likes to be the best at everything!

Did you know?

During each Olympics, the ancient Greeks sacrificed 100 bulls to the god Zeus.

PISTACHIO

A reclusive type, PISTACHIO doesn't say much and likes to hide out in its shell.

Can you find Pistachio?

Honest and loyal, SWORD BEAN is good to have on your side. Plus it has that cool sword, like the samurai warriors of Japan!

True or false?

1. Women could be samurai.   ■ **True**   ■ **False**

2. Samurai would perfume their hair to make it more pleasant for their enemies.   ■ **True**   ■ **False**

3. Dying in battle would be a satisfactory end to a samurai's life.   ■ **True**   ■ **False**

4. The sword is the only weapon a samurai would use.

   ■ **True**   ■ **False**

5. Ninja swords and samurai swords are the same.

   ■ **True**   ■ **False**

How many did you get correct?
Turn this around for the answers below!

Answers:
1. True 2. True 3. True 4. False 5. False

COFFEE BEANS

It's hard to rile up the **COFFEE BEANS**—they never get flustered. They also give great advice.

Advice from the **Coffee Beans**

Q: What should I get Grandma for her birthday?

Slippers!

Q: How can I get my crush to go out with me?

Invite a group to sing karaoke!

Q: Why can't I ever find what I need when I'm leaving the house?

Put your stuff away when you get home!

Q: What should I do for a living?

Pick the skill that will earn the most $$!

Q: Should I buy the new cell phone everyone's talking about?

Wait till you really need a new phone!

SWEET
BEANS

SWEET BEANS are old and wise. Like your grandma and grandpa, but older. And wiser.

Did you know?

Ancient Egyptians slept on pillows made of rock.

Really old stuff

A clam found off the coast of Iceland was determined to be between **405** and **410** years old–Earth's oldest living creature.

The aboriginal fish traps in Brewarrina, New South Wales, Australia, are estimated to be at least **40,000** years old.

The world's oldest living tree is thought to be a 13-foot-tall Norway spruce in Sweden. Scientists say its root system, though not the tree itself, has been growing for **9,550** years.

Three figurines carved from mammoth bone in Germany date back between **30,000** and **33,000** years.

A book of six bound pages of 24-carat gold, written in Etruscan, is more than **2,500** years old. It was discovered in a Bulgarian tomb.

Lima Bean is a know-it-all who doesn't know being a know-it-all can be, you know, irritating.

These beans are American, and they don't speak Japanese very well.

The Jelly Beans are trying to learn Japanese.
Learn with them!

English	Pronunciation in Japanese	Japanese
Good morning.	O-ha-yō	おはよう
Hello!	Kōn-nee-chee-wa	こんにちは
We are American.	Amereeka-jin des	アメリカ人（じん）です
I love New York!	Nyooyōkoo ga dī-sookee	ニューヨークが 大（だい）好（す）き
Hey, did you know?	Neh sheetteroo?	知（し）ってる？
Strawberry	Ee-cheegō	いちご
Grape	Boodō	ぶどう
Orange	Orenjee	オレンジ
Melon	Merun	メロン
Pineapple	Pī-napp-roo	パイナップル
Peach	Mōmō	もも
Raspberry	Razooberee	ラズベリー

THE
SCREAM

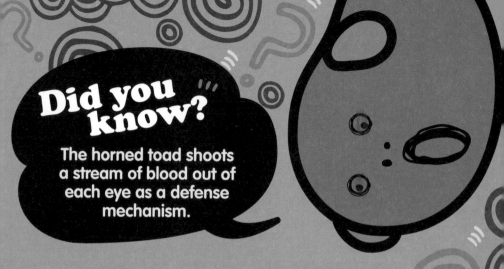

Did you know?

The horned toad shoots a stream of blood out of each eye as a defense mechanism.

THE SCREAM has never really been seen by any bean. Does it really exist? It's a mystery!

Did you know? *The Scream* is the name of a painting by Edward Munch. This Mameshiba is a mung bean.

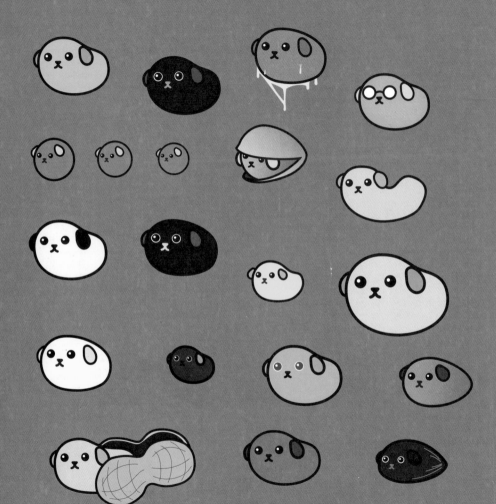